Looking at Lifec

Chicken

Victoria Huseby

FRANKLIN WATTS
LONDON • SYDNEY

This edition 2010

First published in 2007 by Franklin Watts
338 Euston Road, London NW1 3BH

Franklin Watts Australia
Level 17/207 Kent Street
Sydney NSW 2000

Copyright © Franklin Watts 2007

Editor: Rachel Tonkin
Designer: Chris Fraser
Illustrator: John Alston
Picture researcher: Diana Morris
Science consultant: Andrew Solway
Literacy consultant: Gill Matthews

Picture credits:
DK Images: 17; Robert Dowling/Corbis: front cover, 1;
William Gottlieb/Corbis: 21; Julie Habel/Corbis: 5, 15;
Wayne Hutchinson/Photographers Direct: 19;
Peter Kubal/Photographers Direct: 9;
Robert Pickett/Ecoscene: 7, 11, 13.

Every attempt has been made to clear copyright.

Should there be any inadvertent omission please

apply to the publisher for rectification.

A CIP catalogue record for this book
is available from the British Library

ISBN: 978 0 7496 9635 1

Dewey Classification: 636.5P

Printed in Malaysia

Franklin Watts is a division of Hachette Children's Books.

Contents

Laying an egg

A female chicken is called a hen. She makes a **nest** with straw. She lays her **eggs** in the nest. Each egg has a new chicken inside it.

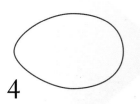

Inside an egg

At first the chicken inside the egg is just a tiny dot. It is called an **embryo**. The yellow **yolk** in the egg has food inside it. This lets the embryo grow.

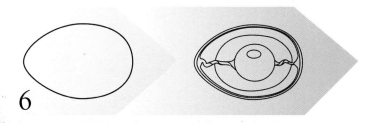

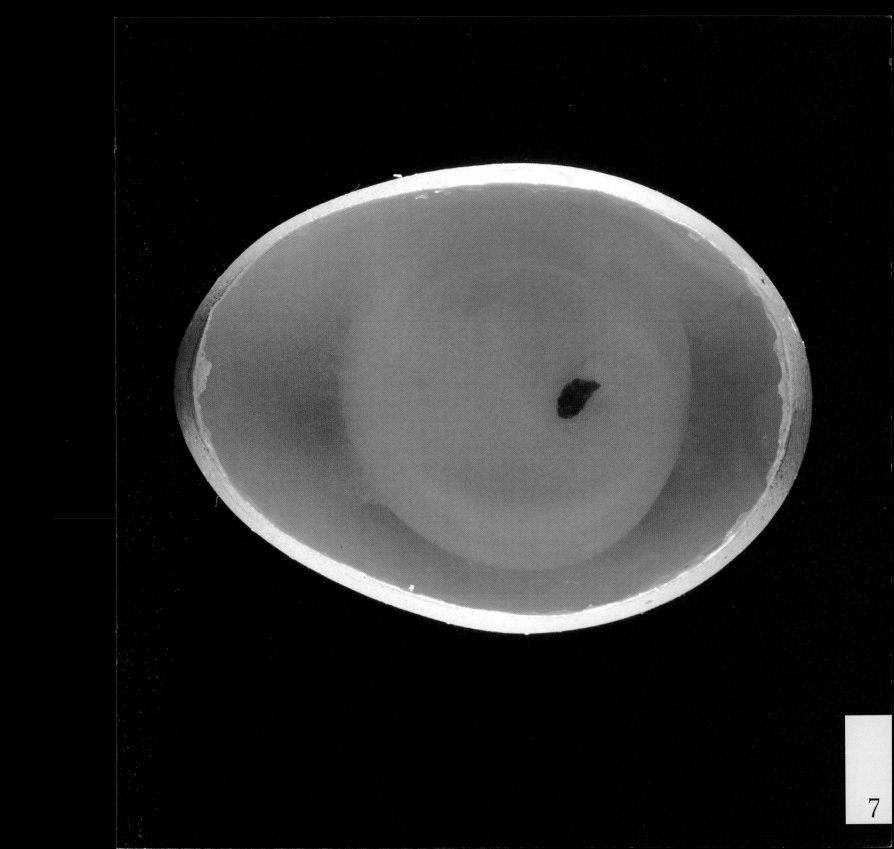

Brooding

The hen helps the embryo to grow by sitting on the eggs. She keeps them warm and safe. This is called **brooding**.

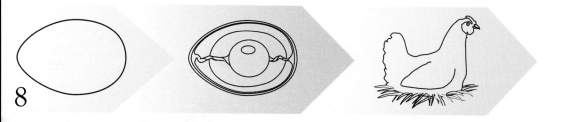

The embryo grows

As the embryo grows it begins to look like a chick. It is protected by a soft, jelly substance called **albumen**. Like the yolk, this has food in it.

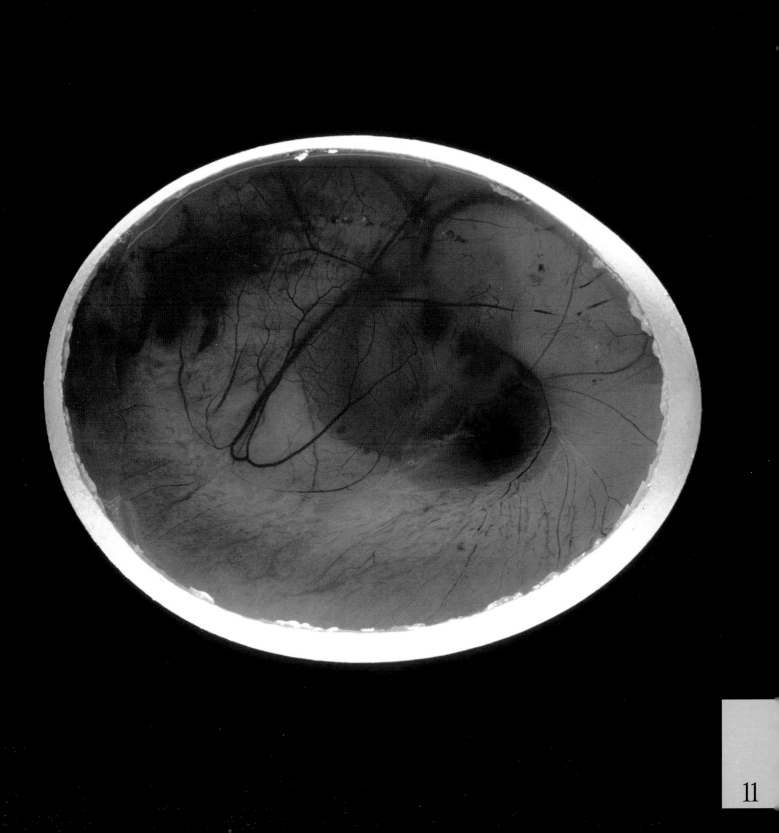

11

Hatching

After three weeks the chick
is ready to hatch. It uses
a special tooth on its beak
called an **egg-tooth** to
break out of the egg.

New chick

The chick soon dries out. It has fluffy yellow **feathers**, called down. The chick can walk as soon as it hatches.

Growing up

As the chick gets older
it grows new feathers.
It starts to look like an
adult chicken.

Adulthood

In a few months the chick is fully grown. Chickens peck the ground looking for food, such as grain and worms.

Making a nest

When a female chicken
is about five months old,
she is ready to lay eggs and
have chicks of her own.

Laying an egg   Inside an egg   Brooding   The embryo grows

20

Hatching → New chick → Growing up → Adulthood

Chicken facts

- There are many different types of chicken. They can be different sizes and colours.

- Only eggs that have been fertilised by a cock will hatch into chicks. The eggs we eat do not have a chick inside them.

- A male chicken is a cock.

- It takes a chicken about 24 hours to make one egg.

- Chickens have wings but they cannot fly far.

- Chickens eat insects, worms, slugs, grain and other things they find in the ground.

- Chickens can lay between 250 and 300 eggs every year.

- Chickens can live for as long as seven years.

Chicken words

Albumen
The white part of the egg which protects the chick as it is growing.

Brooding
When a hen keeps her eggs warm by sitting on them.

Egg
Contains the baby chicken, surrounded by yolk and albumen.

Egg-tooth
A tiny tooth-like point on the tip of a chick's beak. The chick uses the egg-tooth to break out of the egg.

Embryo
The early stage of a young animal before it can move and when it is growing inside an egg or inside its mother.

Feathers
The soft, light and often colourful covering of birds.

Nest
A hollow place built or used by a bird as a home to rear its young.

Yolk
The yellow part of the egg which contains food for the chick.

Index